AMY
the
Hedgehog
Girl

John Coldwell

Illustrated by Caroline Crossland

OXFORD
UNIVERSITY PRESS

Miserable Mr Peck

Her mum was in the kitchen when
Amy rushed in.

'How was school?' asked Mrs Harris,
expecting the usual answer, 'OK.'

'It was great,' cried Amy. 'A lady
gave us a talk on wildlife and she
showed us a hedgehog. I'm going to
become a hedgehog expert.'

'A what?' said Mrs Harris.

'A hedgehog expert. Someone who knows all about hedgehogs.'

'That's good,' said Mrs Harris. 'You'll need to go to the library and see if you can find some books.'

'Oh dear,' Amy groaned. 'I'll have to see Mr Peck.'

Mr Peck was the children's librarian. He was a mean and miserable sort of person. He also lived next door to Amy.

The library was almost empty when Amy arrived. She looked along the shelves, trying to find a book on hedgehogs.

'What are you doing?' snapped a voice behind her.

Amy nearly jumped out of her socks. It was Mr Peck.

'I was looking for a book about animals.'

'Animals, indeed,' sniffed Mr Peck. 'What sort of animals? Tame animals? Wild animals? Animals from Africa? India? Britain?'

'Hedgehogs,' said Amy.

'Hedgehogs!' bawled Mr Peck. 'The very worst animals there are. They dig up vegetables and bite lumps out of them.'

He pulled a book from the shelves.

'If you must study the horrid things, this is the best I can do.'

'Thank you,' said Amy politely.

'Make sure you bring it back on time. And don't you dare bring hedgehogs into your garden. Your garden is next to mine, don't forget. If I see a hedgehog near my carrots, do you know what I am going to do?'

'No,' said Amy.

'I'm going to squirt it with my spray gun.'

At home, Amy read the book on hedgehogs. She found out that they ate slugs and snails. The book didn't say anything about vegetables.

The next day she took the book back to the library.

'What's this?' said Mr Peck. 'This book is not due back for another twenty days.'

'But I've read it,' said Amy. 'Have you got any more books about hedgehogs?'

'Over there,' snapped Mr Peck, pointing with his nose.

Amy walked slowly along the shelves. Where were the books about animals? She was just about to risk asking Mr Peck, when she saw something. It was an old cassette tape, called 'Calls of the Wild'. It looked as if nobody had ever played it.

Amy took it down from the shelf. It was part of a set of animal noises. This was tape number 12 and it was called Hedgehogs.

Amy asked Mr Peck if she could borrow the cassette.

'Of course you can,' he said rudely. 'Though anybody who wants to listen to horrid animal noises must be mad.'

He stamped the cassette box.

'And don't forget to rewind the tape.'

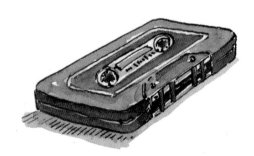

Hedgehog talk

Amy sat in her room listening to the
sounds of hedgehogs on her personal
stereo, over and over again. Amy
repeated the sounds herself.

'I'm talking hedgehog,' thought
Amy. 'I wish I knew what I was saying.
I really need a hedgehog to help me.
I'm sure there's one in the garden. If I
make hedgehog noises, perhaps it will
hear me.'

Amy ran down into the garden and
made hedgehog noises as loudly as she
could.

She stopped and listened, but no
hedgehogs answered. Amy tried again.
But only a cat came into the garden.

'I'm going to keep trying,' said Amy.
'I'm sure I can do it.' At last she got
cold and she went indoors.

The next night Amy tried again. She tried every night for a week.

'What are you doing out there?' asked Mrs Harris.

'Wait and see,' said Amy.

Just then the door bell rang. It was Mr Peck. He stood at the door in his dressing gown. Amy noticed that his hair was wet.

'Mrs Harris,' said Mr Peck. 'Every night when I have my bath I can hear a noise. It seems to be coming from your garden.'

Amy giggled behind her hand.

'Noise?' said Mrs Harris.

'Some sort of animal,' said Mr Peck. 'I'd put poison down if I were you. That is the only way to deal with animals.'

As soon as Mr Peck had gone, Amy dashed out into the garden. 'Mr Peck thought I was an animal,' she said to herself. 'I'm going to try one more time.'

Amy went down on her knees and began to make her hedgehog sounds again.

Almost at once there was a rustling noise and a hedgehog lumbered onto the lawn. Amy was delighted. The hedgehog and Amy snorted and squeaked at each other.

Suddenly a torch beam shone in their eyes.

'What's going on?' said a voice. It was Mr Peck, still in his dressing gown. The hedgehog rolled into a ball.

'I'm chatting to a hedgehog,' said Amy.

'You cheeky young thing. Talking to hedgehogs indeed.'

'Excuse me – ' began Amy.

'And what's more,' Mr Peck cut in, 'hedgehogs are dirty little beasts and they eat up all the vegetables in my garden.'

'Rubbish!' said Amy crossly.
'Hedgehogs are not dirty. And they don't eat vegetables. They eat slugs and snails. Now, if you don't mind, I was talking to a hedgehog.'

Mr Peck was too shocked to answer. His mouth dropped open as Amy snorted gently to the hedgehog. Slowly it unrolled.

A sly look crept across Mr Peck's face.

'How often have you been doing this, my dear?' he asked.

'Never before,' said Amy. 'But from now on, I'll be here every night.'

'Hm,' said Mr Peck. 'You're going to be here every night, you say.'

The amazing hedgehog girl

When Amy came home from school
the next day, Mr Peck was in his front
drive. He was fixing a large board to
the gate. As soon as he saw Amy, he
threw his coat over it.

Amy had promised to show her
mum the hedgehog. It was getting dark
when they stepped into the garden to
see her hedgehog friend.

Amy went down on her knees and began to snort. This time two hedgehogs came up to her.

'What are you talking about?' whispered Mrs Harris.

'Slugs.'

There was a sound from next door. Amy shone her torch towards the fence. There were people staring into her garden. They all had their mouths open.

One person stood out. It was Mr
Peck.

'I've asked a few friends over,' he said
smoothly. 'I hope you don't mind.'

Amy was cross, but she also felt rather
proud that so many people had come to
see her. 'You may watch. But please don't
talk or make a noise. And no photos.'

The people nodded.

Amy went down on her knees and
snorted once more.

This time three more hedgehogs came up. Amy managed to tell the hedgehogs that they had nothing to fear. The people just wanted to see how clever they were. Amy and the hedgehogs talked and played together.

As soon as the hedgehogs had gone, the people behind the fence began to clap and cheer. Of course they wanted to know what Amy and the hedgehogs had been talking about.

'They told me about their young. Then they told me why they curl up into a ball. And where to find the tastiest grubs. Oh, and they told me where they are going to sleep for the winter.'

Mrs Harris hugged Amy.

'You were fantastic,' she said. 'Come in and I'll make you a nice hot drink.'

'Yes. In you go,' said Mr Peck cheerily. 'I'm sure you must be very tired.'

There was something strange about Mr Peck. He had never said anything kind to Amy before. Then she heard an odd noise. It was the sound of coins being dropped into a box.

'It was worth a pound of anybody's money,' she heard someone say.

'Ssh,' said Mr Peck.

Then Amy remembered the board that Mr Peck had been fixing to his front gate. Why had Mr Peck tried to hide it? Amy rushed round to the front of the house. There on the board in large letters it said:

See the Amazing
Hedgehog Girl
Admission only £1·00
(Tea and biscuits)

'What a nerve,' said Amy. Then a
smile crept across her face. 'I know how
to fix you, Mr Peck.'

She raced round to Mr Peck's garden.
Some of the people were still enjoying a
cup of tea and biscuits.

Before Mr Peck could stop her, she said 'Ladies and gentlemen. There is something I must tell you. All the money you have given tonight is going to a hedgehog hospital to look after sick hedgehogs.'

Everyone clapped and nodded their heads. Everyone except Mr Peck. His face went bright red and he made a strange spluttering noise.

'Not only that,' went on Amy, 'but
Mr Peck has agreed that for every
pound that you give tonight, he will
give another pound of his own
money.'

Everyone clapped again and
cheered. Mr Peck went a very pale
colour. Somehow he managed a
smile.

Before he could say anything, Amy said, 'And I am happy to say that the hospital has asked me to take the money for them.'

She held out her hand. Gloomily, Mr Peck passed the box over to Amy.

Then, an even gloomier look spread across his face as he dug into his pocket and pulled out two ten pound notes.

'A big hand for Mr Peck,' said Amy.

This is not quite the end of the
story. Amy felt rather sorry for Mr
Peck.

After she had sent the money to the
hedgehog hospital, she asked the
hedgehogs to patrol Mr Peck's garden.
She told them to make sure that no more
of his vegetables were eaten by slugs.

A few weeks later, Mr Peck won third
prize for his marrows, runner beans and
carrots at the local show.

That evening he leaned over the
fence to show Amy his three prizes.

'It's all thanks to those hedgehogs,'
he said. 'I wish I had known before
how useful they are. I've bought them
a present.'

He handed her one tin of dog food.

'I've just got some new books about
hedgehogs in the library. I read that
they adore dog food,' he explained.

A group of hedgehogs were soon busy tucking in. Amy knelt down beside them.

'What are they saying?' asked Mr Peck.

'Well,' said Amy. 'Hedgehogs are a bit hard to understand when they have their mouths full. But I think they are saying thanks for the dog food.'

'I should think so too,' said Mr Peck. 'I paid a lot of money for that tin. And could you teach them not to speak with their mouths full? It is so rude.'

'I'll try,' said Amy.

She looked at the hedgehogs and smiled.

It seemed to her that they smiled back.

About the author

I was born in London in 1950 and now live by the seaside, in Ramsgate. In the evening I like to write stories and poems. I do this very quietly. Then I go downstairs and play jazz records very loudly. My family think that I do two very daft things. One is going up the garden every night looking for frogs, newts and hedgehogs. The other is supporting Gillingham Football Club.